Non PC World

Published in 2010 by New Holland Publishers (UK) Ltd
London • Cape Town • Sydney • Auckland
Garfield House, 86–88 Edgware Road, London W2 2EA, United Kingdom
80 McKenzie Street, Cape Town 8001, South Africa
Unit 1, 66 Gibbes Street, Chatswood, NSW 2067, Australia
218 Lake Road, Northcote, Auckland, New Zealand

10 9 8 7 6 5 4 3 2

A catalogue record for this book is available from the British Library

ISBN 978 1 84773 714 4

Senior Editor: Kate Parker
Publishing Director: Rosemary Wilkinson
Publisher: Aruna Vasudevan
Design and cover design: Lucy Parissi

Reproduction by Pica Digital PTE Ltd, Singapore
Printed and bound in Italy by L.E.G.O. Spa

Thanks to David Thorne for permission to use his 'Party Invite' piece on
pages 44–47. View more of David's work at www.27bslash6.com.

For more Non PC World please visit us at www.nonpcworld.com or email us
any new funnies at info@nonpcworld.com.

Non PC World

THE INTERNET'S BEST FUNNIES

BEN FRY & ALEC JUPP

NEW
HOLLAND

CONTENTS

WHEN SOMEONE STEALS THE SHOW

I was at Tesco this afternoon, when a lady dropped dead in front of me. I felt really sorry for her – she had just bought a Bag for Life.

You've just popped back from the developers after getting your holiday snaps... but what's that in the background?

HAPPY HOUR!

HE REGRETTED WEARING SANDALS...

NELLE HAD MORE THAN JUST HER TRUNK PACKED

THE NOTORIOUS CAT MOLESTER MAKES HIS FIRST MISTAKE...

SPOT THE SNAKE COMPETITION

THE MUFF RUSTLER STRIKES AGAIN

SHE TURNED UP JUST IN TIME FOR THE WEDDING CAKE

SOME SUNBURNT PLUMS
SPOIL THE PICNIC

A Word of Advice

*Next time you try to look
hot ...flush the toilet*

When being crazy behind closed doors just isn't enough...

SOCCER BALL ★★ signed by either Pele, the former Brazilian soccer player widely renowned by most experts and fans to be the finest player that has ever existed, or by some guy named "Peter". $75. 901-529-

WANTED: Somebody to go back in time with me. This is not a joke. P.O. Box ██, Oakview, CA 93022. You'll get paid after we get back. Must bring your own weapons. Safety not guaranteed. I have only done this once before.

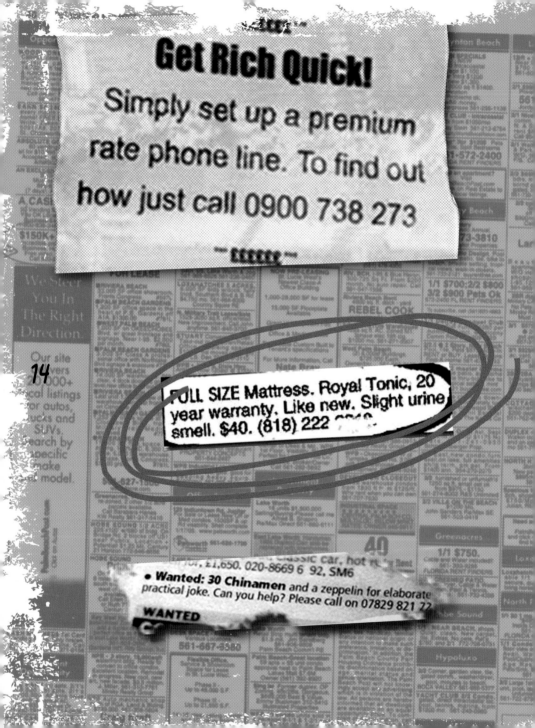

15

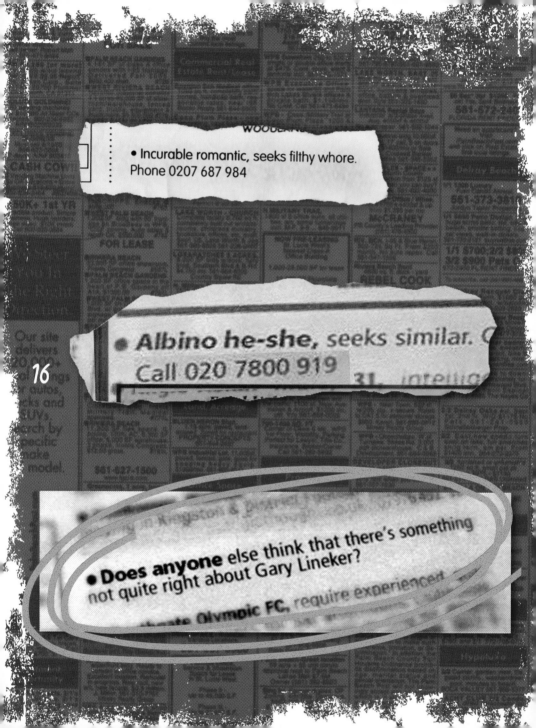

- Incurable romantic, seeks filthy whore. Phone 0207 687 984

- Albino he-she, seeks similar. Call 020 7800 919

16

- Does anyone else think that there's something not quite right about Gary Lineker?

Paddy & Mick went to London to donate sperm. It was a disaster!

Paddy missed the tube & Mick came on the bus!!

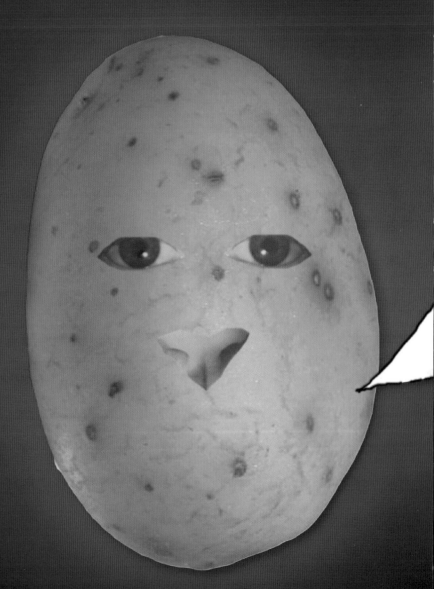

WHAT IS... A BASTARD?

The guy on the right is a member of a bomb squad in the middle of a deactivation.

And the guy on the left? Well, he's a bastard.

WHAT IS... FRIENDSHIP?

"Following the recent financial meltdown and ahead of public
protests in the City of London, banking staff are being
advised to dress down amid fears they will be targeted by
angry demonstrators. One anarchist website has the slogan:
'Burn a banker!'"

Playing with yourself

WHAT IS... A SHOCKER?

24

Quick kids, hide inside Pikachu's vagina!

WHAT IS... THE BENEFIT OF SLAVERY?

It gets stuff done.

WHAT IS… A REAL MAN?

No matter how hard you try, you will never party THIS HARD!

28

This message has not been sent.

To... ben@nonpcworld.com

Cc...

Send

Account ▾   Subject: Serious Warning, - Forward it on.

Hello

Generally, I hate the warnings that get sent around but I have to admit that this one is '_serious_'.

Please protect everyone you know by sending this to your entire email list.

Basically, someone comes to your front door and says they are conducting a survey and asks you to show them your bum.

Do NOT show them your bum - it is a scam. They only want to see your bum.

I wish I'd got this yesterday,

I feel so stupid and cheap....

Dear Deirdre,

I have never written asking for your help before, but I really need your advice.

I have suspected for some time now that my wife has been cheating on me.

The usual signs; phone rings but if I answer, the caller hangs up.

My wife has been going out with 'the girls' a lot recently although when I ask their names she always says, 'just some friends from work, you don't know them.' I try to stay awake and look out for her when she comes home, but I usually fall asleep.

Anyway, I have never broached the subject with my wife.

I think deep down I just did not want to know the truth, but last night she went out again and I decided to finally check on her.

Around midnight, I hid in the garage behind my golf clubs so I could get a good view of the whole street when she arrived home from a night out with 'the girls'. When she got out of the car she was buttoning up her blouse, which was open, and she took her panties out of her purse and slipped them on.

It was at that moment, crouching behind my golf clubs, that I noticed a hairline crack where the grip meets the graphite shaft on my 3-wood.

Is this something I can fix myself or should I take it back to the pro-shop where I bought it?

32

A NOTE FROM MUM YOU WON'T FORGET.

Boys
There was cum
in the plughole of the Shower.
whoever is wanking in the shower
Stop it NOW
its fucking DISGUSTING
do it in your own damn
rooms.
MUM

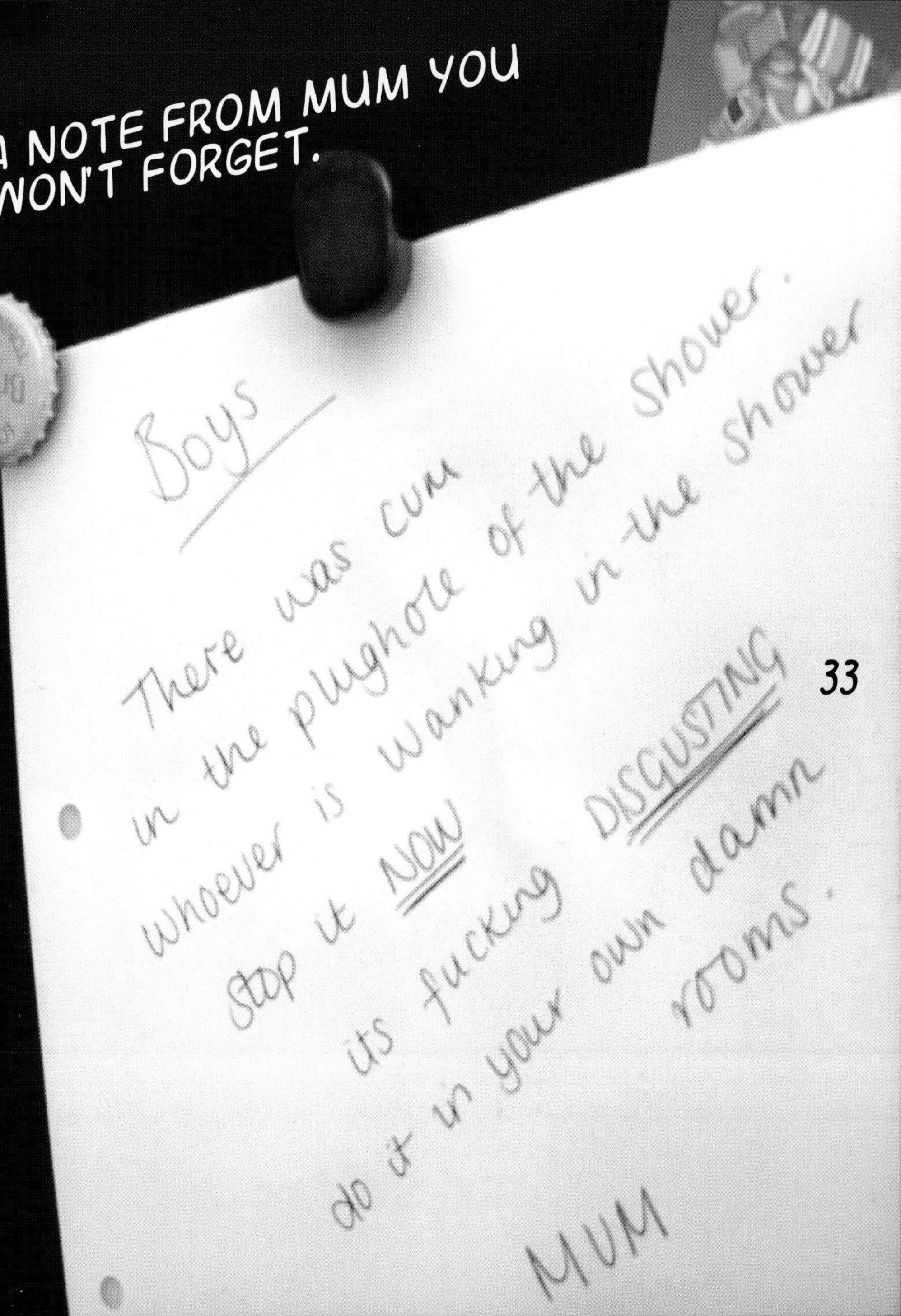

If you can't find the book you want, maybe it's the...

WONG FOOK HING BOOK STORE

A Chinese takeaway owner walks into an exchange bureau to get some euros for his holiday in Spain. He asks for £100 worth and gets 120 euros in return.

A couple of days later he realises he needs more money and goes back in to get another hundred quid's worth and gets 110 euros back this time.

'Why you only give me 110 euro for £100 when 2 day ago you give me 120?'

'Fluctuations'

'Fluck you white people too!

A HEARTWARMING STORY

In 1986, Peter Davies was on a hike through the bush when he came across a young bull elephant standing with one leg raised in the air.

The elephant seemed distressed, so Peter approached it very carefully. He got down on one knee, inspected the elephant's foot, and found a large piece of wood deeply embedded in it. As carefully and as gently as he could, Peter worked the wood out with his knife, after which the elephant gingerly put down its foot. The elephant turned to face the man, and with a rather curious look on its face, stared at him for several tense moments.

Peter stood frozen, thinking of nothing else but being trampled. Eventually the elephant trumpeted loudly, turned, and walked away. Peter never forgot that elephant or the events of that day.

Twenty years later, Peter was walking through the Chicago Zoo with his teenage son. As they approached the elephant enclosure, one of the creatures turned and walked over to near where Peter and his son Cameron were standing. The large bull elephant stared at Peter, lifted its front foot off the ground, and then put it down. The elephant did that several times then trumpeted loudly, all the while staring at the man. Remembering the encounter in 1986, Peter could not help wondering if this was the same elephant. Peter summoned up his courage, climbed over the railing, and made his way into the enclosure. He walked right up to the elephant and stared back in wonder. The elephant trumpeted again, wrapped its trunk around one of Peter legs and slammed him against the railing, killing him instantly.

Probably wasn't the same elephant.

Drop acid, not bombs.

The Fonz's hair is perfect as usual

The Force is strong in this one.

Leave the money on
the dresser, Big Boy

Dogtanian

A man walks up to a woman in his office and tells her that her hair smells nice.

The woman immediately goes into her supervisor's office and tells him that she wants to file a sexual harassment suit and explains why.

The supervisor is puzzled, "What's wrong with your co-worker telling you your hair smells nice?"

The woman replies, "He's a midget."

Dear Connie,

I know the counsellor said we shouldn't contact each other during our "cooling off" period, but I couldn't wait anymore. The day you left, I swore I'd never talk to you again. But that was just the wounded little boy in me talking. Still, I never wanted to be the first one to make contact.

In my fantasies, it was always you who would come crawling back to me. I guess my pride needed that. But now I see that my pride's cost me a lot of things. I'm tired of pretending I don't miss you. I don't care about looking bad anymore. I don't care who makes the first move as long as one of us does. Maybe it's time we let our hearts speak as loudly as our hurt. And This is what my heart says: "There's no one like you, Connie." I look for you in the eyes and breasts of every woman I see, but they're not you.

They're not even close. Two weeks ago, I met this girl at Flamingos and brought her home with me. I don't say this to hurt you, but just to illustrate the depth of my desperation.She was young, maybe 19; with one of those perfect bodies that only youth and maybe a childhood spent ice skating can give you. I mean, just a perfect body. Tits like you wouldn't believe and an ass that just wouldn't quit. Every man's dream, right? But as I sat on the couch being blown by this stunner, I thought, look at the stuff we've made important in our lives. It's all so superficial. What does a perfect body mean? Does it make her a better person? Does she have a better heart than my yes, but you see what I'm getting at. Does it make her a better in bed? Well, In this case, moderately attractive Connie? I doubt it. And I'd never really thought of that before.

I don't know, maybe I'm just growing up a little. Later, after I'd tossed her about a half a pint of throat yoghurt, I found myself thinking, "Why do I feel so drained and empty?" It wasn't just her flawless technique or her slutty, shameless hunger, but something else. Some nagging feeling of loss. Why did it feel so incomplete? And then it hit me. It didn't feel the same because you weren't there to watch. Do you know what I mean? Nothing feels the same without you. Jesus, Connie, I'm just going crazy without you. And everything I do just reminds me of you.

Do you remember Carol, that single mom we met at the Holiday Inn Lounge last year? Well, she dropped by last week with a pan of lasagne. She said she figured I wasn't eating right without a woman around. I didn't know what she meant till later, but that's not the real story.Anyway, we had a few glasses of wine and the next thing you know, we're banging away in our old bedroom. And this tart's a total monster in the sack. She's giving me everything, you know, like a real woman does when she's not hung up about her weight or her career and whether the kids can hear us. And all of a sudden, she spots that tilting mirror on your grandmother's old vanity. So she puts it on the floor and we straddle it, right, so we can watch ourselves. And it's totally hot, but it makes me sad. Cause I can't help thinking, "Why didn't Connie ever put the mirror on the floor? We've had this old vanity for what, 14 years, and we never used it as a sex toy."

Saturday, your sister drops by with my copy of the restraining order.I mean, Vicky's just a kid and all, but she's got a pretty good head on her shoulders and she's been a real friend to me during this painful time.She's given me lots of good advice about you and about women in general. She's pulling for us to get back together, Connie, she really is. So we're doing Jell-O shots in a hot bubble bath and talking about happier times. Here's this teenage girl with the same DNA as you and all I can do is think of how much she looked like you when you were 18. And that just about makes me cry. And then it turns out Vicky's really into the whole anal thing, that gets me to thinking about how many times I pressured you about trying it and how that probably fuelled some of the bitterness between us. But do you see how even then, when I'm thrusting inside your baby sister's cinnamon ring, all I can do is think of you? It's true, Connie. In your heart you must know it. Don't you think we could start over? Just wipe out all the grievances away and start fresh? I think we can.

If you feel the same please, please, please let me know. Otherwise, Can you let me know where the remote is.

Love, Mitch.

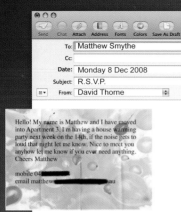

Dear Matthew,
Thank you for the party invite. At first glance I thought it may be a child's party what with it being vibrant and having balloons but I realise you probably did your best with what little tools were available. I wouldn't miss it for the world. What time would you like me there?

Regards, David.

Hi David
Sorry the note was just to let you know that we might be a bit loud that night. The house warming is really just for friends and family but you can drop past for a beer if you like.

Cheers Matthew

44

Thanks Matthew,
Including me in your list of friends and family means a lot. You and I don't tend to have long discussions when we meet in the hallway and I plan to put a stop to that. Next time we bump into each other I intend to have a very long conversation with you and I am sure you are looking forward to that as much as I am. I have told my friend Ross that you are having a party and he is as excited as I am. Do you want us to bring anything or will everything be provided?

Regards, David.

Hi David
As I said, my housewarming is just for friends and family. There is not a lot of room so cant really have to many people come. Sorry about that mate.

Cheers Matthew

New Message

To: Matthew Smythe
Cc:
Bcc: Monday 8 Dec 2008
Subject: Re: Re: Re: Re: R.S.V.P.
From: David Thorne

Dear Matthew,
I can appreciate that, our apartments are not very large are they? I myself like to go for a jog every night to keep fit but fear leaving the house so I have to jog on the spot taking very small steps with my arms straight down. I understand the problems of space restrictions all too well. If you would like to store some of your furniture at my place during the party you are quite welcome to - if we move your cane furniture into my spare room for the night and scatter cushions on the ground, that would provide a lot more seating and create a cozy atmosphere at the same time. I have a mirror ball that you can borrow. I have told Ross not to invite anyone else due to the space constraints so it will just be us two and my other friend Simon. When I told Simon that Ross and I were going to a party he became quite angry that I had not invited him as well so I really didn't have any choice as he can become quite violent. Sometimes I am afraid to even be in the same room as him. So just myself Ross and Simon. Simon's girlfriend has a work function on that night but might come along after that if she can get a lift with friends.

Regards, David.

New Message

To: David Thorne
Cc:
Bcc: Monday 8 Dec 2008
Subject: Re: Re: Re: Re: Re: R.S.V.P.
From: Matthew Smythe

Wtf? Nobody can come to the houswarming party it is just for friends and family. I dont even know these people. How do you know I have cane furniture? Are you the guy in apartment 1?

New Message

Send Chat Attach Address Fonts Colors Save As Draft Photo Browser Show Stationery

To: Matthew Smythe
Cc:
Date: Monday 8 Dec 2008
Subject: Re: Re: Re: Re: Re: Re: R.S.V.P.
From: David Thorne

Hi Matthew,

I understand it is an exclusive party and I appreciate you trusting my judgement on who to bring. I just assumed you have cane furniture, doesn't everybody? Cane is possibly one of the most renewable natural resources we have after plastic, it is not only strong but lightweight and attractive. Every item in my apartment is made of cane, including my television. It looks like the one from Gilligan's Island but is in colour of course. Do you remember that episode where a robot came to the island? That was the best one in my opinion. I always preferred Mary Anne to Ginger, same with Flintstones - I found Betty much more attractive than Wilma but then I am not really keen on redheads at all. They have freckles all over their body did you know? It's the ones on their back and shoulders that creep me out the most.

Anyway, Ross rang me today all excited about the party and asked me what the theme is, I told him that I don't think there is a theme and we discussed it and feel that it should be an eighties themed party. I have a white suit and projector and am coming as Nik Kershaw. I have made a looping tape of 'wouldn't it be good' to play as I am sure you will agree that this song rocks and has stood the test of time well. I am in the process of redesigning your invites appropriately and will get a few hundred of them printed off later today. I will have to ask you for the money for this as print cartridges for my Epson are pretty expensive. They stopped making this model a month after I bought it and I have to get the cartridges sent from China. Around $120 should cover it. You can just pop the money in my letter box if I don't see you before tonight.

Regards, David

New Message

Send Chat Attach Address Fonts Colors Save As Draft

To: David Thorne
Cc:
Bcc: Monday 8 Dec 2008
Subject: Re: Re: Re: Re: Re: Re:Re: R.S.V.P.
From: Matthew Smythe

What the fuck are yout alking about? There is no theme for the party it is just a few friends and family. noone else can come IT IS ONLY FOR MY FRIENDS AND FAMILY do you understand? Do not print anything out because I am not paying for something I dont need and didnt ask you to do! look I am sorry but i am heaps busy and that night is not convenient. Are you in Apatrment1?

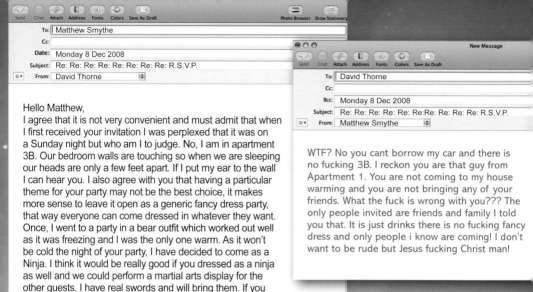

To: Matthew Smythe
Cc:
Date: Monday 8 Dec 2008
Subject: Re: Re: Re: Re: Re: Re: Re: Re: R.S.V.P.
From: David Thorne

Hello Matthew,

I agree that it is not very convenient and must admit that when I first received your invitation I was perplexed that it was on a Sunday night but who am I to judge. No, I am in apartment 3B. Our bedroom walls are touching so when we are sleeping our heads are only a few feet apart. If I put my ear to the wall I can hear you. I also agree with you that having a particular theme for your party may not be the best choice, it makes more sense to leave it open as a generic fancy dress party, that way everyone can come dressed in whatever they want. Once, I went to a party in a bear outfit which worked out well as it was freezing and I was the only one warm. As it won't be cold the night of your party, I have decided to come as a Ninja. I think it would be really good if you dressed as a ninja as well and we could perform a martial arts display for the other guests. I have real swords and will bring them. If you need help with your costume let me know, I have made mine by wrapping a black t-shirt around my face with a hooded jacket and cut finger holes in black socks for the gloves. I do not have any black pants so will spray paint my legs on the night.

It is a little hard to breathe in the costume so I will need you to keep the window open during the party to provide good air circulation. Actually, I just had a thought, how awesome would it be if I arrived 'through' the window like a real ninja. We should definitely do that. I just measured the distance between our balconies and I should be able to jump it. I once leaped across a creek that was over five metres wide and almost made it.

Also, you mentioned in your invitation that if there was anything I needed, to let you know. My car is going in for a service next week and I was wondering, seeing as we are good friends now, if it would be ok to borrow yours on that day. I hate catching the bus as they are full of poor people who don't own cars.

Regards, David.

New Message

To: David Thorne
Cc:
Bcc: Monday 8 Dec 2008
Subject: Re: Re: Re: Re: Re: Re:Re: Re: Re: Re: R.S.V.P.
From: Matthew Smythe

WTF? No you cant borrow my car and there is no fucking 3B. I reckon you are that guy from Apartment 1. You are not coming to my house warming and you are not bringing any of your friends. What the fuck is wrong with you??? The only people invited are friends and family I told you that. It is just drinks there is no fucking fancy dress and only people i know are coming! I don't want to be rude but Jesus fucking Christ man!

47

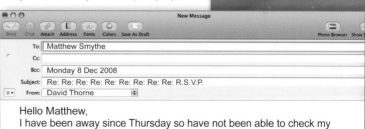

New Message

To: Matthew Smythe
Cc:
Bcc: Monday 8 Dec 2008
Subject: Re: Re: Re: Re: Re: Re: Re: Re: Re: R.S.V.P.
From: David Thorne

Hello Matthew,

I have been away since Thursday so have not been able to check my email from home. Flying back late today in time for the party and just wanted to say that we are really looking forward to it. Will probably get there around eleven or twelve, just when it starts to liven up. Simon's girlfriend Cathy's work function was cancelled so she can make it after all which is good news. She will probably have a few friends with her so they will take the minivan. Also, I have arranged a Piñata.

Regards, David.

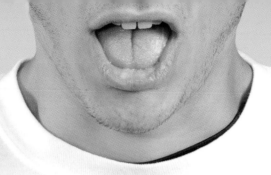

THE T-SHIRT COMPETITION

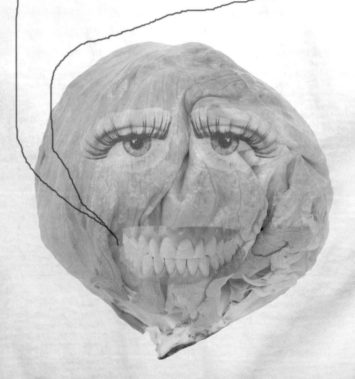

I met a 14 year old girl on the internet.
She was clever, funny, flirty and sexy,
so I suggested we meet up. She turned out
to be an undercover detective.

How cool is that at her age?

I SURVIVED NEVERLAND

5. BUT DON'T MAKE ME
TALK ABOUT IT

4. RUDOLF'S GONNA GET FISTED TONIGHT

50

3. A RAY OF HOPE

2. BUT I STILL ENJOYED MYSELF

1. I ALSO BRING MY OWN LUNCH

DESPITE RUMOURS, THE NHS IS IN RUDE HEALTH

THE KEY WEST BODY PAINT COMPETITION
AND THE WINNERS ARE....

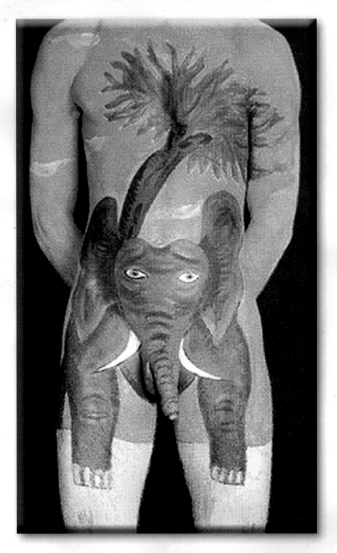

MALE

FEMALE

They Said What?

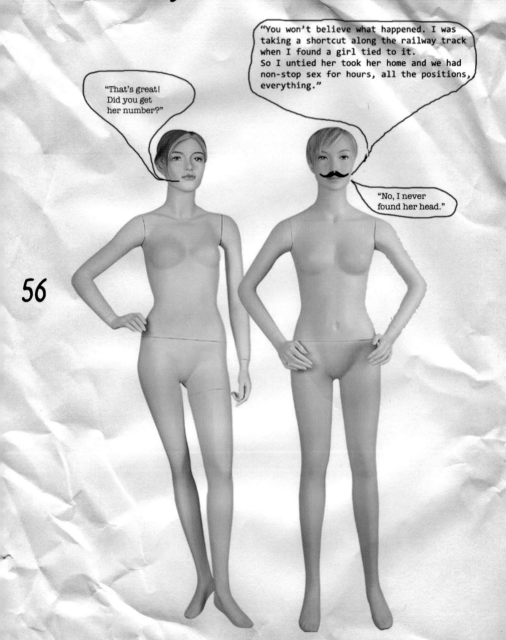

Dear landlord...

1. **'This is to let you know that our lavatory seat is broken and we can't get BBC2'**

2. 'It's all the dog mess that I find hard to swallow.'

3. **'... and their 18-year-old son is continually banging his balls against my fence.'**

4. 'Will you please send someone to mend the garden path? My wife tripped and fell on it yesterday and now she is pregnant.'

5. **'50% of the walls are damp, 50% have crumbling plaster and 50% are just plain filthy.'**

6. 'The toilet is blocked and we cannot bathe the children until it is cleared.'

7. **'I want to complain about the farmer across the road; every morning at 6am his cock wakes me up and it's now getting too much for me.'**

8. 'Our kitchen floor is damp. We have two children and would like a third, so please send someone round to do something about it.'

9. **'I want some repairs done to my cooker as it has backfired and burnt my knob off.'**

10. 'I am writing on behalf of my sink, which is coming away from the wall.'

57

LATE SHOW (BBC MIDLANDS)

Alex Trelinski: What is the capital of Italy ?

Contestant: France.

Trelinski: France is another country. Try again.

Contestant: Oh, um, Benidorm.

Trelinski: Wrong, sorry, let's try another question. In which country is the Parthenon?

Contestant: Sorry, I don't know.

Trelinski: Just guess a country then.

Contestant: Paris.

JAMES O'BRIEN SHOW (LBC)

James O'Brien: How many kings of England have been called Henry?

Contestant: Er, well, I know there was a Henry the Eighth ... Er. Er ... Three?

ROCK FM (PRESTON)

Presenter: Name a film starring Bob Hoskins that is also the name of a famous painting by Leonardo da Vinci.

Contestant: 'Who Framed Roger Rabbit?'

UNIVERSITY CHALLENGE (BBC2)

Jeremy Paxman: What is another name for 'cherry pickers' and 'cheese mongers'?

Contestant: Homosexuals.

Jeremy Paxman: No. They're regiments in the British Army who will be very upset with you

UNIVERSITY CHALLENGE (BBC2)

Bamber Gascoigne: What was Gandhi's first name?

Contestant: Goosey?

Lost in translation

A vicar books into a hotel and says to the hotel clerk "I hope the porn channel in my room is disabled."

"No sir", She replies, "it's just regular porn, you sick bastard"

62

汤力水
Tonic Water ¥:15.00

干姜水
Fuck The Ginger Water ¥:15.00

健怡可乐
Pesi-Cola ¥:15.00

可口可乐
Coca-Cola ¥:10.00

64

一旦失窃要报警，切莫姑息又养奸

If you are stolen, call the police at once.

上海市公安局城市轨道交通分局
Urban Mass Transportation Branch Shanghai Public Security Bureau

This cute mild curry uses 100% Japanese apple and cheerful hamster.

ハムモンドカレー

リンゴとハムスターのアジのあるキュートなカレー

残疾人专用
Special for deformed

Fresh herpes
0.95
Molokhia
2.75
Spring onion
2.95

66

Clairvoyant's Meeting - See Your Future

Friday 8th September
Nailsworth Villlage hall
8pm

One Night Only

CANCELLED DUE TO UNFORESEEN CIRCUMSTANC

Have you ever wondered at your own abilities to read situations?
Have you ever 'had a gut feeling' that turned out ot be right?
Then this is the night for you, unlock your true potential......

Guest speaker Sean 'The Eye' Baird

Refreshements will be served afterwards

68

CAUTION

THIS SIGN HAS

SHARP EDGES

DO NOT TOUCH THE EDGES OF THIS SIGN

ALSO, THE BRIDGE IS OUT AHEAD

NO HOOKING ANYTIME

THIS IS A NO HOOKING ZONE. YOU ARE BEING RECORDED AND WILL BE REPORTED. YOUR VEHICLE CAN BE TAKEN AWAY.

NOTICE

PLEASE DO NOT
BRING YOUR
DOG TO
SHIT HERE !

Baboons

STOP
HAMMERTIME!

Directive 000189: When working with naked flames, wear only flame retardant clothing and the protective masks provided.

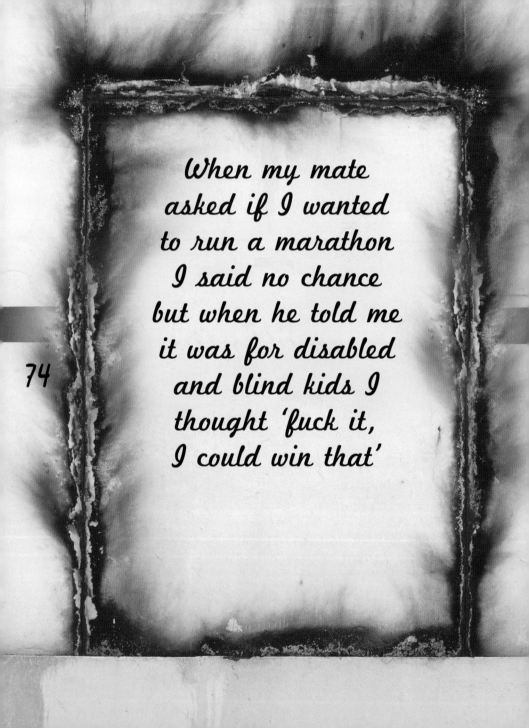

When my mate
asked if I wanted
to run a marathon
I said no chance
but when he told me
it was for disabled
and blind kids I
thought 'fuck it,
I could win that'

Directive 000689: Visitors are required to wear protective clothing and/or use the special safety equipment that has been provided.

Directive 000956: Use only protective equipment that has been provided for hazardous work.

Budget.

PERTH RESERVATIONS HOTLINE 13 27 27
COUNTRY CALLERS 1300 305 888

Hi,
My name is Jack
I accidently hit your
car & someone saw me
so I'm pretending to
right down my details.
SORRY.
Jack

What do you expect from someone who can't spell 'write'?

Carrier pigeon delivers

Radical penis
reduction technique

Even Cookies have bad days

What's that
noise? Quick,
get the
camera!

Bathroom store
toilet vandalised

Two reasons why it's so hard to solve a Redneck murder:

1. The DNA all matches.

2. There are no dental records.

The story of Adam and Steve

82

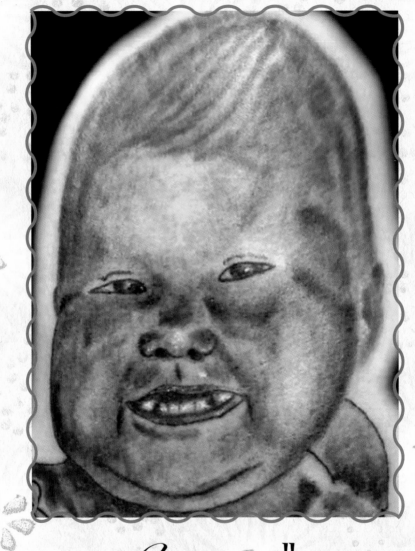

Coochy koo!!

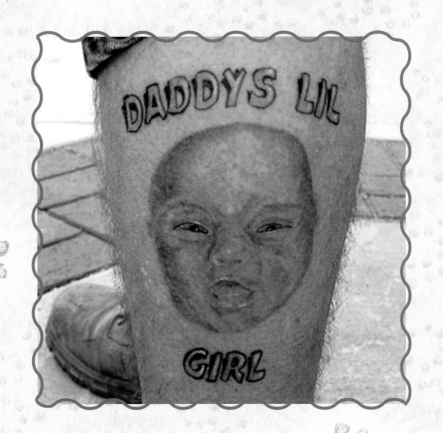

Daddy's angry little alien!

Was there a
3-fingered discount?

Now you'll never forget what they looked like!

86

Baywatch meets Crimewatch

87

The removal specialist
recommended exorcism

88

I wanna make love to
you like a reptile

I went into my local dvd rental shop and asked could I rent a copy of Batman Forever.

The guy behind the counter said, "No you'll have to bring it back"

What do you call a Mexican Peeping Tom?

Señor Minge

The middle one please – lots of mustard, no onions

What a Cock!

The first date was going well

And you thought
it was just
trapped wind...

Wassup!!
Well, er, not
your tits

93

She regretted not having a caesarian

Hi! My name's Count C**t!

Don't mess. He's menstrual.

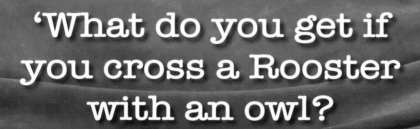

'What do you get if you cross a Rooster with an owl?

'A cock that stays up all night.'

96